D0855904

Benedict XVI

Marian Thoughts

BENEDICT XVI

Marian Thoughts

SELECTION OF TEXTS
BY POPE BENEDICT XVI
EDITED BY LUCIO COCO

Introduction by
Fr. Ermes Maria Ronchi, osm

Illustrated in Color

CATHOLIC BOOK PUBLISHING CORP.
New Jersey

NIHIL OBSTAT: Rev. Msgr. James M. Cafone, M.A., S.T.D.
Censor Librorum

IMPRIMATUR: ✠ Most Rev. John J. Myers, J.C.D., D.D.
Archbishop of Newark

This translation of *Pensieri Mariani*, first published in Italian, is published by arrangement with The K.S. Giniger Company, Inc. (English translation supervised by Kate Marcellin-Rice.)

Icons of the Virgin Mary © Monastery Icons—
www.monasteryicons.com

(T-120)

ISBN 978-0-89942-117-9

CONTENTS

INTRODUCTION

THE living tent of the Word. With this image that condenses biblical memory and expressive beauty, Benedict XVI evokes in his typical language the central position of the Blessed Virgin's experience in history (*Homily,* May 26, 2005). She is the humble tent of the Word, moved only by the breath of the Spirit, where God's exodus to us begins and ends.

The collection of Marian thoughts edited by Lucio Coco outlines a successful narrative magisterium that traces the pilgrimage of Mary, motivated throughout her life by the first joyful prophecy: *kaire, rejoice,* faithful all her days to the long echo of the "yes" of the Annunciation.

This selection brings out the newest and most effective characteristics of Pope Benedict's use of language: sobriety, lucidity, and beauty. The Pope's discourse on Mary is brief but does not miss a single essential point. His strategic positioning of Mary within theology is precise: the meaning of her life is "[to magnify] the Lord" (cf. Lk 1:46), not to fulfill her own plan but as part of a greater design.

He reawakens attention to beauty, a powerful means of intuiting and of speaking, a force of the heart that creates all communion and "restores enchantment" to life.

And you will discover here a continuous reference to Mary the joyous believer, already bound by the first words of the Angel to that joy which is an essential noun in Christianity, one of the names of man, far from the false, sad forms of asceticism that divide body and spirit, mind and heart.

Thus, for every member of the faithful, to name Mary, a joyful believer, is equivalent to feeling comforted in life.

Living tent of the Word: Mary, the meeting place of the human and the divine, the point where time and eternity converge. These words contain the Pontiff's tireless emphasis on the vital link between God and man: more divinity means more humanity: *only if God is great is man also great.*

Holy Mary, *a woman of courage and wonder,* showed in her life this increase of humanity, this expansion of the heart that is granted to those who totally fulfill Christianity. But this is not all; in this exchange of gifts, as the Pope says in a new and incisive phrase, now, with Mary's Assumption, *"Heaven has a heart."*

The biblical memory of Mary opens with a house in which it is an Angel who speaks and ends with a house, the Upper Room in Jerusalem, in which it is wind and fire that speak: *in her, the home of the Word and "at home" with the Word* (cf. *Homily,* August 15, 2005), each person rediscovers himself or herself as a tent in which the homeless Merciful One seeks a home. The *Virgin with the open heart* (cf. *Angelus,* September 10, 2006) shows that God is not deserved but rather is welcomed.

Mary, the Church in her nascent state, becomes a teacher of Christianity: Pope Benedict cogently says that Mary *learned* Jesus: *"through the long, ordinary years of the hidden life, as she brought up Jesus, or when at Cana in Galilee she asked for the first sign, or when finally on Calvary, by the Cross, she looked on Jesus, she 'learned' Him moment by moment"* (*Address,* May 26, 2006).

Thus going to Mary is going to *a school of Christianity,* learning from her the alphabet of faith and hope.

"Mary" is one of the words most full of hope. And love. Love that enters events in its entirety, that goes to the heart of things with a regal step, that does not protect but exposes, unarmed yet immensely strong.

Even the prayers to Mary that conclude this collection do not present a static and abstract image but a dynamic presence: just as she was committed to the Christ event, so she is now committed to the Christian event. She cares for us in God's eternity as a mother who has gone ahead, who precedes us but at the same time waits for us, who slows her step, keeping pace with ours in order not to overtake us. Thus, in Mary's footsteps, it becomes invigorating to imagine and live faith as an open and supportive rather than a closed system.

In Mary the small and the infinite converge: in the events of daily life, in eyes that marvel at things, in love under every silence, in the poetry of familiar gestures, in hope under every fear, in the instant that shines in eternity, and in eternity that infiltrates into the instant, *Mary wants . . . to teach us a way of life in which God is acknowledged as the center of all there is* (*Angelus,* September 10, 2006), she wants to teach us not to live without mystery; because those who find God find life in its fullness.

The promise of the Angel is very concrete: *you will conceive and give birth.* Mary is the authoritative witness that God enters life and transforms it. In her, in her body—which is the place where the heart is located—the line of the visible and the line of the invisible in the History of Salvation meet.

She is, in her body, the crossroads, one of the meeting places between the materiality of life and God. In her body and in her faith, Mary refers tirelessly to the center of faith: Jesus Christ, the shining witness that God comes and transforms the body and life, that the divine comes and makes the human flourish.

Ermes Maria Ronchi

1. Holy Mary

WE do not praise God sufficiently by keeping silent about His Saints, especially Mary, "the Holy One" who became His dwelling place on earth. The simple and multiform light of God appears to us exactly in its variety and richness only in the countenance of the Saints, who are the true mirrors of His light.

And it is precisely by looking at Mary's face that we can see more clearly than in any other way the beauty, goodness, and mercy of God. In her face we can truly perceive the divine light.

Homily, August 15, 2006

1. The Annunciation

2. The Virgin of Advent

A T a crucial time in history, Mary offered herself, her body and soul, to God as a dwelling place. In her and from her the Son of God took flesh. Through her the Word was made flesh (cf. Jn 1:14). Thus, it is Mary who tells us what Advent is: going forth to meet the Lord Who comes to meet us; waiting for Him, listening to Him, looking at Him.

Mary tells us why church buildings exist: they exist so that room may be made within us for the Word of God; so that within us and through us the Word may also be made flesh today. *Homily,* December 10, 2006

3. Mary Immaculate

I N today's consumer society, this period [Advent] has unfortunately suffered a sort of commercial "pollution" that risks changing its authentic spirit, marked by recollection, moderation, and joy, which is not external but intimate. It is thus providential that almost as a portal to Christmas there should be the feast of the one who is the Mother of Jesus and who, better than anyone else, can lead us to know, love, and adore the Son of God made man.

Let us therefore allow her to accompany us; may her sentiments prompt us to prepare ourselves with heartfelt sincerity and openness of spirit to recognize in the Child of Bethlehem the Son of God Who came into the world for our redemption. Let us walk together with her in prayer and accept the repeated invitation that the Advent liturgy addresses to us to remain in expectation—watchful and joyful expectation—for the Lord will not delay: He comes to set His people free from sin.

Angelus, December 11, 2005

4. In God's Hands

THIS is something we should indeed learn on the day of the Immaculate Conception: the person who abandons himself totally in God's hands does not become God's puppet, a boring "yes man"; he does not lose his freedom. Only the person who entrusts himself totally to God finds true freedom, the great, creative immensity of the freedom of good.

The person who turns to God does not become smaller but greater, for through God and with God he becomes great, he becomes divine, he becomes truly himself. The person who puts himself in God's hands does not distance himself from others, withdrawing into his private salvation; on the contrary, it is only then that his heart truly awakens and he becomes a sensitive, hence, benevolent and open person.

Homily, December 8, 2005

5. Listening

"REVERENTIAL hearing." This attitude was typical of Mary Most Holy, as the icon of the Annunciation symbolically portrays: the Virgin receives the heavenly Messenger while she is intent on meditating upon the Sacred Scriptures, usually shown by a book that Mary holds in her hand, on her lap or on a lectern. . . . Mary [is the] humble handmaid of the divine word." *

Angelus, November 6, 2005

6. Our Example

THE Virgin is the One who continues to listen, always ready to do the Lord's will; she is an example for the believer who lives in search of God.

Angelus, December 4, 2005

---

*In the original the Pope says: "Let us pray that like Mary, the Church will be a humble handmaid of the divine word."]

7. Hail Mary

THE first word on which I would like to meditate with you is the Angel's greeting to Mary. In the [English] translation the Angel says: "Hail, Mary." But the Greek word below, "Kaire," means in itself "be glad" or "rejoice." . . .

This is the first word that resounds in the New Testament as such, because the Angel's announcement to Zechariah of the birth of John the Baptist is the word that still rings out on the threshold between the two Testaments. It is only with this dialogue, which the Angel Gabriel has with Mary, that the New Testament really begins.

We can therefore say that the first word of the New Testament is an invitation to joy: "rejoice, be glad!" The New Testament is truly "Gospel," the "Good News" that brings us joy. God is not remote from us, unknown, enigmatic, or perhaps dangerous. God is close to us, so close that He makes Himself a child and we can informally address this God.

Homily, December 18, 2005

8. Full of Grace

"*F*ULL of grace" . . . is Mary's most beautiful name, the name God Himself gave to her to indicate that she has always been and will always be the *beloved*, the elect, the one chosen to welcome the most precious gift, Jesus: "the incarnate love of God" (*Deus Caritas Est*, 12).

Angelus, December 8, 2006

9. Loved by the Lord

"*F*ULL of grace—*gratia plena*," which in the original Greek is *kecharitōménē* . . . , "beloved" of God (cf. Lk 1:28). . . . It is a title expressed in passive form, but this "passivity" of Mary, who has always been and is for ever "loved" by the Lord, implies her free consent, her personal and original response.

In *being loved*, in receiving the gift of God, Mary is fully *active*, because she accepts with personal generosity the wave of God's love poured out upon her. In this too, she is the perfect disciple of her Son, Who realizes the fullness of His freedom and thus exercises the freedom through obedience to the Father.

Homily, March 25, 2006

10. The Lord Be with You

GOD, Who became present here on earth, truly dwells in Mary. Mary becomes His tent. What all the cultures desire—that God dwell among us—is brought about here.

St. Augustine says: "Before conceiving the Lord in her body she had already conceived Him in her soul." She had made room for the Lord in her soul and thus really became the true Temple where God made Himself incarnate, where He became present on this earth.

Homily, August 15, 2006

11. The Tent of the Lord

MARY, Mother of the Lord, truly teaches us what entering into communion with Christ is: Mary offered her own flesh, her own blood to Jesus and became a living tent of the Word, allowing herself to be penetrated by His presence in body and spirit.

Let us pray to her, our holy Mother, so that she may help us to open our entire being, always more, to Christ's presence; so that she may help us to follow Him faithfully, day after day, on the streets of our life.

Homily, May 26, 2005

12. "Do Not Fear, Mary" [Lk 1:30]

"**D**O not fear, Mary," he [the Angel] says. In fact, there was reason for her to fear, for it was a great burden to bear the weight of the world upon herself, to be the Mother of the universal King, to be the Mother of the Son of God: what a burden that was!

It was too heavy a burden for human strength to bear! But the Angel said: "Do not fear! Yes, you are carrying God, but God is carrying you. Do not fear!" *Homily,* December 18, 2005

13. . . . And in the Hour of Our Death

"**D**O not fear": Mary also addresses these words to us. . . . This world of ours is a world of fear: the fear of misery and poverty, the fear of illness and suffering, the fear of solitude, the fear of death. We have in this world a widely developed insurance system; it is good that it exists.

But we know that at the moment of deep suffering, at the moment of the ultimate loneliness of death, no insurance policy will be able to protect us. The only valid insurance in those moments is the one that comes to us from the Lord, Who also assures us: "Do not fear, I am always with you." We can fall, but in the end we fall into God's hands, and God's hands are good hands. *Homily,* December 18, 2005

14. I am the servant of the Lord

MARY belonged to that part of the People of Israel who in Jesus' time were waiting with heartfelt expectation for the Savior's coming. . . . She could not, however, have imagined how this coming would be brought about. Perhaps she expected a coming in glory. The moment when the Archangel Gabriel entered her house and told her that the Lord, the Savior, wanted to take flesh in her, wanted to bring about His coming through her, must have been all the more surprising to her.

We can imagine the Virgin's apprehension. Mary, with a tremendous act of faith and obedience, said "yes": "I am the servant of the Lord." And so it was that she became the "dwelling place" of the Lord, a true "temple" in the world and a "door" through which the Lord entered upon the earth.

Homily, November 26, 2005

15. Woman of Hope

MARY is a woman of hope: only because she believes in God's promises and awaits the salvation of Israel can the Angel visit her and call her to the decisive service of these promises.

Encyclical, Deus Caritas Est, 41

16. Let it be done to me according to your word

A T the end of the colloquium, Mary answered the Angel, "I am the servant of the Lord. Let it be done to me according to your word." Thus, Mary anticipated the "Our Father's" third invocation: "Your will be done." She said "yes" to God's great will, a will apparently too great for a human being; Mary said "yes" to this divine will, she placed herself within this will, placed her whole life with a great "yes" within God's will, and thus opened the world's door to God.

Adam and Eve, with their "no" to God's will, had closed this door. "Let God's will be done": Mary invites us too to say this "yes," which sometimes seems so difficult. We are tempted to prefer our own will, but she tells us: "Be brave, you too say: 'Your will be done,' because this will is good."

It might at first seem an unbearable burden, a yoke impossible to bear; but in reality, God's will is not a burden; God's will gives us wings to fly high and thus we too can dare, with Mary, to open the door of our lives to God, the doors of this world, by saying "yes" to His will, aware that this will is the true good and leads us to true happiness.   *Homily*, December 18, 2005

17. Handmaid of the Lord

[MARY] is and remains the handmaid of the Lord who does not put herself at the center, but wants to lead us toward God, to teach us a way of life in which God is acknowledged as the center of all there is and the center of our personal lives.

Angelus, September 10, 2006

18. Giving Herself Entirely

[MARY] is, so to speak, totally emptied of herself; she has given herself entirely to Christ and with Him is given as a gift to us all. Indeed, the more the human person gives himself, the more he finds himself.

Homily, December 8, 2005

19. A Dwelling Place in Heaven

WE can praise Mary, we can venerate Mary for she is "blessed," she is blessed for ever. . . . She is blessed because she is united to God, she lives with God and in God. On the eve of His Passion, taking leave of His disciples, the Lord said: "In My Father's house are many rooms. . . . I go to prepare a place for you." By saying, "I am the handmaid of the Lord; let it be done to me according to your word," Mary prepared God's dwelling here on earth; with her body and soul, she became His dwelling place and thereby opened the earth to heaven.

Homily, August 15, 2006

20. A Flame of Love

[M]ARY teaches us that] to love according to God it is necessary to live in Him and of Him: God is the first "home" of human beings, and only by dwelling in God do men and women burn with a flame of divine love that can set the world "on fire."

Message, April 29, 2006

21. The Call

MARY received her vocation from the lips of an Angel. The Angel does not enter our room visibly, but the Lord has a plan for each of us: He calls each one of us by name.

Our task is to learn how to listen, to perceive His call, to be courageous and faithful in following Him and, when all is said and done, to be found trustworthy servants who have used well the gifts given us.

Homily, September 11, 2006

2. The Visitation

22. On a Visit

MARY went to see her elderly cousin Elizabeth—whom everyone said was sterile but who instead had reached the sixth month of a pregnancy given to her by God (cf. Lk 1:36)—carrying in her womb the recently conceived Jesus. She was a young girl but she was not afraid, for God was with her, within her. . . .

Jesus' presence filled her with the Holy Spirit. When she entered Elizabeth's house, her greeting was overflowing with grace: John leapt in his mother's womb, as if he were aware of the coming of the One Whom he would one day proclaim to Israel. The children exulted, the mothers exulted.

This meeting, imbued with the joy of the Holy Spirit, is expressed in the Canticle of the *Magnificat*.

Address, May 31, 2005

23. Mary and Elizabeth

THE hidden protagonist in the meeting between the young Mary and the by-then elderly Elizabeth is Jesus. Mary bears Him in her womb as in a sacred tabernacle and offers Him as the greatest gift to Zechariah, to Elizabeth, his wife, and also to the infant developing in her womb.

"Behold," the Mother of John the Baptist says, "when the voice of your greeting came to my ears, the babe in my womb leaped for joy" (Lk 1:44). Whoever opens his or her heart to the Mother encounters and welcomes the Son and is pervaded by His joy.

Address, May 31, 2005

24. A Woman of Faith

ELIZABETH, the mother of John the Baptist, reserved the first Beatitude in the Gospel [for Mary]: "Blessed is she who believed that there would be a fulfillment of what was spoken to her from the Lord" (Lk 1:45). Mary is the "believer" par excellence, the pure and perfect woman of faith.

cf. General Audience, February 15, 2006
[cf. *I Salmi dei Vespri,* Libreria Vaticana
Editrice 2006, p. 488]

25. The Journey of Joy

JOY must always be shared. Joy must be communicated. Mary went without delay to communicate her joy to her cousin Elizabeth. . . . This is the real commitment of Advent: to bring joy to others. Joy is the true gift of Christmas, not expensive presents that demand time and money. We can transmit this joy simply: with a smile, with a kind gesture, with some small help, with forgiveness.

Let us give this joy, and the joy given will be returned to us. Let us seek in particular to communicate the deepest joy, that of knowing God in Christ. Let us pray that this presence of God's liberating joy will shine out in our lives.

Homily, December 18, 2005

26. Bringing Jesus to Others

YES, welcoming Jesus and bringing Him to others is the true joy of Christians! Dear brothers and sisters, let us follow and imitate Mary, a deeply Eucharistic soul, and our whole life can become a *Magnificat* (cf. *Ecclesia de Eucharistia,* 58), praise of God. May this be the grace that we ask from the Virgin Most Holy. . . .

Address, May 31, 2005

27. Eucharistic Existence

A T the school of Mary, "Woman of the Eucharist," as the late Pope John Paul II loved to call her, we welcome Jesus' living presence in ourselves to bring Him to everyone by loving service.

Let us learn to always live in communion with the Crucified and Risen Christ, allowing ourselves to be led by His and our heavenly Mother. In this way, nourished by the Word and Bread of Life, our existence will become entirely Eucharistic and thanks will be given to the Father through Christ in the Holy Spirit.

Angelus, May 29, 2005

28. Model of the Church

T HE first thing that Mary did after receiving the Angel's message was to go "in haste" to the house of her cousin Elizabeth in order to be of service to her (cf. Lk 1:39). The Virgin's initiative was one of genuine charity; it was humble and courageous, motivated by faith in God's Word and the inner promptings of the Holy Spirit.

Those who love forget about themselves and place themselves at the service of their neighbor. Here we have the image and model of the Church! Every Ecclesial Community, like the Mother of Christ, is called to accept with total generosity the mystery of God Who comes to dwell within her and guides her steps in the ways of love.

Homily, March 25, 2006

3. The Magnificat

29. My Soul Magnifies the Lord

OUTSTANDING among the saints is Mary, Mother of the Lord and mirror of all holiness. In the Gospel of Luke we find her engaged in a service of charity to her cousin Elizabeth, with whom she remained for "about three months" (Lk 1:56) so as to assist her in the final phase of her pregnancy.

"Magnificat anima mea Dominum," she says on the occasion of that visit, "My soul magnifies the Lord" (Lk 1:46). In these words she expresses her whole program of life: not setting herself at the center, but leaving space for God, who is encountered both in prayer and in service of neighbor—only then does goodness enter the world.

Mary's greatness consists in the fact that she wants to magnify God, not herself. She is lowly: her only desire is to be the handmaid of the Lord (cf. Lk 1:38, 48). She knows that she will only contribute to the salvation of the world if, rather than carrying out her own projects, she places herself completely at the disposal of God's initiatives.

Deus Caritas Est, 41

30. My Soul Proclaims
the Greatness of the Lord

IN the Gospel we heard the *Magnificat*, that great poem inspired by the Holy Spirit that came from Mary's lips, indeed, from Mary's heart. This marvelous canticle mirrors the entire soul, the entire personality of Mary. We can say that this hymn of hers is a portrait of Mary, a true icon in which we can see her exactly as she is. . . .

It begins with the word *"Magnificat"*: my soul "magnifies" the Lord, that is, "proclaims the greatness" of the Lord. Mary wanted God to be great in the world, great in her life and present among us all. She was not afraid that God might be a "rival" in our life, that with His greatness He might encroach on our freedom, our vital space.

She knew that if God is great, we too are great. Our life is not oppressed but raised and expanded: it is precisely then that it becomes great in the splendor of God. . . . Only if God is great is humankind also great. With Mary, we must begin to understand that this is so.

Homily, August 15, 2005

31. Thinking with God

MARY'S poem—the *Magnificat*—is quite original; yet at the same time, it is a "fabric" woven throughout of "threads" from the Old Testament, of words of God. Thus, we see that Mary was, so to speak, "at home" with God's word, she lived on God's word, she was penetrated by God's word.

To the extent that she spoke with God's words, she thought with God's words, her thoughts were God's thoughts, her words, God's words. She was penetrated by divine light and this is why she was so resplendent, so good, so radiant with love and goodness.

Mary lived on the Word of God, she was imbued with the Word of God. And the fact that she was immersed in the Word of God and was totally familiar with the Word also endowed her later with the inner enlightenment of wisdom. Those who think with God think well, and those who speak to God speak well. They have valid criteria to judge all the things of the world. They become prudent, wise, and at the same time good; they also become strong and courageous with the strength of God, Who resists evil and fosters good in the world.

Homily, August 15, 2005

32. Dwelling Place of the Word

[M]ARY] lives her whole life in the Word of God. It is as though she were steeped in the Word. Thus, all her thoughts, her will, and her actions are imbued with and formed by the Word. Since she herself dwells in the Word, she can also become the new "Dwelling Place" of the Word in the world.

Address, March 11, 2006

33. Willing with God

THE *Magnificat*—a portrait, so to speak, of [Mary's soul]—is entirely woven from threads of Holy Scripture, threads drawn from the Word of God. Here we see how completely at home Mary is with the Word of God; with ease she moves in and out of it.

She speaks and thinks with the Word of God; the Word of God becomes her word, and her word issues from the Word of God. Here we see how her thoughts are attuned to the thoughts of God, how her will is one with the will of God.

Deus Caritas Est, 41

34. A Woman of Charity

"MARY . . . is a woman who loves. . . . As a believer who in faith thinks with God's thoughts and wills with God's will, she cannot fail to be a woman who loves" (*Deus Caritas Est*, 41).

Yes, dear brothers and sisters, Mary is the fruit and sign of the love God has for us, of his tenderness and mercy. Therefore, together with our brothers in the faith of all times and all places, we turn to her in our needs and hopes, in the joyful and sorrowful events of life.

Address, May 1, 2006

35. Daring with God

[M]ARY'S] heart was enlarged by being and feeling together with God. In her, God's goodness came very close to us. Mary thus stands before us as a sign of comfort, encouragement, and hope.

She turns to us, saying: "Have the courage to dare with God! Try it! Do not be afraid of Him! Have the courage to risk with faith! Have the courage to risk with goodness! Have the courage to risk with a pure heart! Commit yourselves to God; then you will see that it is precisely by doing so that your life will become broad and light, not boring but filled with infinite surprises, for God's infinite goodness is never depleted!"

Homily, December 8, 2005

36. Mary's Humility

WHY exactly did God choose from among all women Mary of Nazareth? The answer is hidden in the unfathomable mystery of the divine will. There is one reason, however, which is highlighted in the Gospel: her humility. . . . In the *Magnificat*, her canticle of praise, the Virgin herself says: "My soul magnifies the Lord . . . because He looked upon His servant in her lowliness" (Lk 1:46, 48).

Yes, God was attracted by the humility of Mary, who found favor in His eyes (cf. Lk 1:30). She thus became the Mother of God, the image and model of the Church, chosen among the peoples to receive the Lord's blessing and communicate it to the entire human family.

Angelus, December 8, 2006

37. Marian Praise

IN the *Magnificat*, the great hymn of Our Lady . . . , we find some surprising words. Mary says: "Henceforth all generations will call me blessed." The Mother of the Lord prophesies the Marian praises of the Church for all of the future, the Marian devotion of the People of God until the end of time.

In praising Mary, the Church did not invent something "adjacent" to Scripture: she responded to this prophecy that Mary made at that moment of grace.

Homily, August 15, 2006

4. Christmas

38. Christmas

TO transform the world, God chose a humble young girl from a village in Galilee, Mary of Nazareth, and challenged her with this greeting: "Hail, full of grace, the Lord is with you." In these words lies the secret of an authentic Christmas. God repeats them to the Church, to each one of us: Rejoice, the Lord is close!

With Mary's help, let us offer ourselves with humility and courage so that the world may accept Christ, Who is the source of true joy.

Angelus, December 17, 2006

39. Motherhood of Mary

THE mother is the one who gives life but also who helps and teaches how to live. Mary is a Mother, the Mother of Jesus, to Whom she gave her blood and her body. And it is she who presents to us the eternal Word of the Father, Who came to dwell among us.

Homily, December 31, 2005

40. The Theotokos

IN the passage from the Letter to the Galatians that we have just heard, St. Paul said: "God sent forth His Son, born of woman" (Gal 4:4). Origen commented: "Note well that he did not say, 'born *by means* of a woman' but 'born *of* a woman' "(*Comment on the Letter to the Galatians, PG* 14, 1298).

This acute observation of the great exegete and ecclesiastical writer is important: in fact, if the Son of God had been born only "by means of" a woman, He would not truly have taken on our humanity, something that instead He did by taking flesh "of" Mary. Mary's motherhood, therefore, is true and fully human.

The fundamental truth about Jesus as a divine Person who fully assumed our human nature is condensed in the phrase: "God sent forth His Son born of woman." He is the Son of God, He is generated by God, and *at the same time* He is the son of a woman, Mary. He comes from her. He is *of* God and *of* Mary. For this reason one can and must call the Mother of Jesus the Mother of God . . . [in Greek, *Theotokos*].

Homily, December 31, 2006

41. "Glory to God
in the highest . . . " [Lk 2:14]

"HAIL, Holy Mother," the liturgy sings, "the Child to Whom you gave birth is the King of Heaven and Earth for ever." The Angels' proclamation at Bethlehem resounds in Mary's motherly heart, filling it with wonder: "Glory to God in the highest, and peace on earth to those on whom His favor rests" (Lk 2:14). And the Gospel adds that Mary "treasured all these things and reflected on them in her heart" (Lk 2:19).

Like Mary, the Church also treasures and reflects upon the Word of God, comparing it to the various changing situations she encounters on her way.

Angelus, January 1, 2006

42. "and peace on earth to those on whom His favor rests." [Lk 2:14]

WHO are those whom God loves, and why does He love them? Does God have favorites? Does He love only certain people, while abandoning the others to themselves? The Gospel answers these questions by pointing to some particular people whom God loves . . . Mary, Joseph, Elizabeth, Zechariah, Simeon and Anna . . . the shepherds and the Wise Men from the East, the "Magi." . . .

They were people who were watchful . . . , ready to receive God's Word through the Angel's proclamation. Their life was not closed in on itself; their hearts were open. In some way, deep down, they were waiting for something; they were waiting for God. Their watchfulness was a kind of readiness—a readiness to listen and to set out. They were waiting for a light that would show them the way.

That is what is important for God. He loves everyone, because everyone is His creature. But some persons have closed their hearts; there is no door by which His love can enter. They think that they do not need God, nor do they want Him.

Other persons, who, from a moral standpoint, are perhaps no less wretched and sinful, at least experience a certain remorse. They are waiting for God. They realize that they need His goodness, even if they have no clear idea of what this means. Into their expectant hearts God's light can enter, and with it, His peace. God seeks persons who can be vessels and heralds of His peace.

Let us pray that He will not find our hearts closed. Let us strive to be active heralds of His peace—in the world of today.

Homily, December 24, 2005

43. Virgin Mother

THE Christian community, which in these days has remained in prayerful adoration before the crib, looks with particular love to the Virgin Mary, identifying itself with her while contemplating the newborn Baby, wrapped in swaddling clothes and laid in a manger.

Like Mary, the Church also remains in silence in order to welcome and keep the interior resonances of the Word made flesh and in order not to lose the divine-human warmth that radiates from His presence. The Church, like the Virgin, does none other than show Jesus, the Savior, to everyone, and reflects to each one the light of His face, the splendor of goodness and truth.

Angelus, January 1, 2007

44. Bringing forth Christ

IF, according to the flesh, the Mother of Christ is one alone, according to the faith all souls bring forth Christ; each, in fact, welcomes the Word of God within. . . . [Ambrose, *Exposition of the Holy Gospel according to Saint Luke,* 2:26-27]. . . . Thus, interpreting Our Lady's very words, the Holy Doctor invites us to ensure that the Lord can find a dwelling place in our own souls and lives.

Not only must we carry Him in our hearts, but we must bring Him to the world, so that we too can bring forth Christ for our epoch. Let us pray the Lord to help us praise Him with Mary's spirit and soul, and to bring Christ back to our world.

General Audience, February 15, 2006

45. Spiritual incarnation

"IN the first [coming]," St. Bernard wrote, "Christ was our redemption; in the last coming He will reveal Himself to us as our life: in this lies our repose and consolation" (*Discourse 5 on Advent, 1*).

The archetype for that coming of Christ, which we might call a "spiritual incarnation," is always Mary. Just as the Virgin Mother pondered in her heart the Word made flesh, so every individual soul and the entire Church are called during their earthly pilgrimage to wait for Christ Who comes and to welcome Him with faith and love ever new.

Homily, December 2, 2006

46. Vocation and mission

[M ARY] welcomed Jesus with faith and gave Him to the world with love. This is also our vocation and our mission, the vocation and mission of the Church: to welcome Christ into our lives and give Him to the world, so "that the world might be saved through Him" (Jn 3:17).

Angelus, December 8, 2006

47. The face of the Child

M AY Mary help us to recognize in the face of the Child of Bethlehem, conceived in her virginal womb, the divine Redeemer Who came into the world to reveal to us the authentic face of God.

Angelus, December 4, 2005

48. The face of God

W HO can accompany us better on this demanding journey of holiness than Mary? Who can teach us to adore Christ better than she? May she help especially the new generations to recognize the true face of God in Christ and to worship, love and serve Him with total dedication.

Angelus, August 7, 2005

49. Epiphany of the Lord

"HOW can this come about?" we also ask ourselves with the words that the Virgin addresses to the Archangel Gabriel. And she herself, the Mother of Christ and of the Church, gives us the answer: with her example of total availability to God's will—*"Let it be done to me according to your word."* (Lk 1:38)—she teaches us to be a "manifestation" of the Lord, opening our hearts to the power of grace and faithfully abiding by the words of her Son, light of the world and the ultimate end of history.

Homily, January 6, 2006

50. Presentation of Jesus at the Temple

THE first person to be associated with Christ on the path of obedience, proven faith and shared suffering was His Mother, Mary. The Gospel text portrays her in the act of offering her Son: an unconditional offering that involves her in the first person.

Mary is the Mother of the One Who is "the glory of [His] people Israel" and a "light for revelation to the Gentiles," but also "a sign that is spoken against" (cf. Lk 2:32, 34). And in her immaculate soul, she herself was to be pierced by the sword of sorrow, thus showing that her role in the history of salvation did not end in the mystery of the Incarnation but was completed in loving and sorrowful participation in the death and Resurrection of her Son.

Bringing her Son to Jerusalem, the Virgin Mother offered Him to God as a true Lamb Who takes away the sins of the world. She held Him out to Simeon and Anna as the proclamation of redemption; she presented Him to all as a light for a safe journey on the path of truth and love.

Homily, February 2, 2006

51. Simeon's prophecy

IN the words of the elderly Simeon [cf. Lk 2:34-35] . . . together with salvation [are anticipated] the contradictory sign of the Cross, and the sword that beneath the Cross of the Son was to pierce the Mother's soul, thereby making her not only the Mother of God but also Mother of us all.

Address, May 1, 2006

52. The vocations of Mary

WE contemplate [Mary] on the Memorial of her Presentation in the Temple as Mother and model of the Church, who welcomes in herself both vocations: to virginity and to marriage, to contemplative life and to active life.

Angelus, November 19, 2006

53. Mary Kept All These Things in Her Heart [Lk 2:52]

THE Evangelist Luke describes [Mary] as the silent Virgin who listens constantly to the eternal Word, who lives in the Word of God. Mary treasures in her heart the words that come from God and, piecing them together as in a mosaic, learns to understand them. Let us too, at her school, learn to become attentive and docile disciples of the Lord.

Homily, January 1, 2006

54. Virgin of Silence

LET us ask the Virgin Mary to teach us the secret of silence that becomes praise, of recollection that is conducive to meditation, of love for nature that blossoms in gratitude to God. Thus, we will more easily be able to welcome the light of the Truth into our hearts and practice it in freedom and love.

Angelus, July 17, 2005

5. Disciple of Jesus

55. At Cana of Galilee

"THEY have no wine" (Jn 2:3). Weddings in the Holy Land were celebrated for a whole week; the entire town took part, and consequently much wine was consumed. Now the bride and groom find themselves in trouble, and Mary simply says this to Jesus. She doesn't ask for anything specific, much less that Jesus exercise His power, perform a miracle, produce wine. She simply hands the matter over to Jesus and leaves it to Him to decide about what to do.

In the simple words of the Mother of Jesus, then, we can see . . . her affectionate concern for people, that maternal affection that makes her aware of the problems of others. We see her heartfelt goodness and her willingness to help.

This is the Mother that generations of people come [on pilgrimage] to visit. To her we entrust our cares, our needs, and our troubles. Her maternal readiness to help, in which we trust, appears here for the first time in the Holy Scriptures.

Homily, September 11, 2006

56. Do Whatever He Tells You [Jn 2:5]

IT is worth going a little deeper, not only to understand Jesus and Mary better, but also to learn from Mary the right way to pray. Mary does not really ask something of Jesus: she simply says to Him: "They have no wine" (Jn 2:3). . . . Mary leaves everything to the Lord's judgment.

At Nazareth she gave over her will, immersing it in the will of God: "I am the servant of the Lord; let it be with me according to your word" (Lk 1:38). And this continues to be her fundamental attitude. This is how she teaches us to pray: not by seeking to assert before God our own will and our own desires, however important they may be, however reasonable they might appear to us, but rather to bring them before Him and to let Him decide what He intends to do.

From Mary we learn graciousness and readiness to help, but we also learn humility and generosity in accepting God's will, in the confident conviction that, whatever it may be, it will be our, and my own, true good.

Homily, September 11, 2006

57. Our Advocate

[A T Cana of Galilee] Mary, the Mother of the Lord . . . received from the faithful the title of *Advocate:* she is our advocate before God. And this is how we see her, from the wedding-feast of Cana onward: as a woman who is kindly, filled with maternal concern and love, a woman who is attentive to the needs of others and, out of desire to help them, brings those needs before the Lord. . . .

Homily, September 12, 2006

58. The Intercession of Mary

[A T Cana of Galilee] in response to the request of His Mother Mary, Jesus comes to the help of the spouses in difficulty by transforming the water into wine. Mary also intercedes with Jesus for us. Her strong faith is our model. We must entrust our requests to her motherly intercession.

Angelus, Greeting in German, January 14, 2007

59. "Learning" Jesus

MARY learned from Jesus! From her very first *"fiat,"* through the long, ordinary years of the hidden life, as she brought up Jesus, or when at Cana in Galilee she asked for the first sign, or when finally on Calvary, by the Cross, she looked on Jesus, she "learned" Him moment by moment. Firstly in faith and then in her womb, she received the Body of Jesus and then gave birth to Him.

Day after day, enraptured, she adored Him. She served him with solicitous love, singing the *Magnificat* in her heart. . . . Let Mary guide you as you "learn" Jesus. Keep your eyes fixed on Him. Let Him form you.

Address, May 26, 2006

60. Christ at the Center

HOW necessary it is—both for the lives of individuals and for the serene and peaceful coexistence of all people—to see God as the center of all there is and the center of our personal lives. The supreme example of this attitude is Mary, Mother of the Lord. Throughout her earthly life, she was the Woman who listened, the Virgin whose heart was open toward God and toward others. . . .

She is and remains the handmaid of the Lord who does not put herself at the center, but wants to lead us toward God, to teach us a way of life in which God is acknowledged as the center of all there is and the center of our personal lives.

Angelus, September 10, 2006

61. Public Life

WE can imagine how in various situations the Virgin must have pondered those words [of the Angel: "Do not fear, Mary" (Lk 1:30)], and must have heard them again. At the moment when Simeon said to her: "This Child is destined to be the downfall and the rise of many in Israel, a sign that will be opposed—and you yourself will be pierced with a sword," at that very moment in which she might have succumbed to fear, Mary returned to the Angel's words and felt their echo within her: "Do not fear; God is carrying you."

Then, when contradictions were unleashed against Jesus during His public life and many said, "He is crazy," she thought once again of the Angel's words in her heart; "Do not fear," and went ahead. Lastly, in the encounter on the way to Calvary and then under the Cross, when all seemed to be destroyed, she again heard the Angel's words in her heart: "Do not fear." Hence, she stood courageously beside her dying Son and, sustained by faith, moved toward the Resurrection, toward Pentecost, toward the foundation of the new family of the Church.

Homily, December 18, 2005

62. Listening to Christ

THE Virgin Mary herself, among all human creatures the closest to God, still had to walk day after day in a pilgrimage of faith (cf. *Lumen Gentium,* n. 58), in her heart constantly guarding and meditating on the Word that God addressed to her through Holy Scripture and through the events of the life of her Son, in Whom she recognized and welcomed the Lord's mysterious voice. And so, this is the gift and duty for each one of us . . . to listen to Christ, like Mary. To listen to Him in His Word, contained in Sacred Scripture. To listen to Him in the events of our lives, seeking to decipher in them the messages of Providence.

Finally, to listen to Him in our brothers and sisters, especially in the lowly and the poor, for whom Jesus Himself demands our concrete love. To listen to Christ and obey His voice: this is the principal way, the only way, that leads to the fullness of joy and of love.

Angelus, March 12, 2006

6. By the Cross

63. On Calvary

THE traditional image of the Crucifixion . . . portrays the Virgin Mary at the foot of the Cross, according to the description of the Evangelist John, the only one of the Apostles who stayed by the dying Jesus. . . .

The Evangelist recounts: Mary was standing by the Cross (cf. Jn 19:25-27). Her sorrow is united with that of her Son. It is a sorrow full of faith and love. The Virgin on Calvary participates in the saving power of the suffering of Christ, joining her "fiat," her "yes," to that of her Son.

Angelus, September 17, 2006

64. The Sorrowful Virgin

IN [Mary] God has impressed His own image, the image of the One Who follows the lost sheep even up into the mountains and among the briars and thornbushes of the sins of this world, letting Himself be spiked by the crown of thorns of these sins in order to take the sheep on His shoulders and bring it home.

As a merciful Mother, Mary is the anticipated figure and everlasting portrait of the Son.

Thus, we see that the image of the Sorrowful Virgin, of the Mother who shares her suffering and her love, is also a true image of the Immaculate Conception.

Homily, December 8, 2005

65. The Legacy of Jesus

IN today's Gospel we have heard how the Lord gave Mary as a Mother to the beloved disciple and, in him, to all of us. In every age, Christians have received with gratitude this legacy of Jesus, and, in their recourse to His Mother, they have always found the security and confident hope that gives them joy in God and makes us joyful in our faith in Him.

May we too receive Mary as the lodestar guiding our lives, introducing us into the great family of God! Truly, those who believe are never alone.

Homily, September 12, 2006

66. Our Mother

THE lives of the Saints are not limited to their earthly biographies but also include their being and working in God after death. In the Saints one thing becomes clear: those who draw near to God do not withdraw from men, but rather become truly close to them. In no one do we see this more clearly than in Mary. The words addressed by the crucified Lord to His disciple—to John and through him to all disciples of Jesus: "Behold, your mother!" (Jn 19:27)—are fulfilled anew in every generation.

Mary has truly become the Mother of all believers. Men and women of every time and place have recourse to her motherly kindness and her virginal purity and grace, in all their needs and aspirations, their joys and sorrows, their moments of loneliness, and their common endeavors.

Deus Caritas Est, 42

67. Mary's Mission

MARY'S motherhood, which began with her *fiat* in Nazareth, is fulfilled at the foot of the Cross. Although it is true—as St. Anselm says—that "from the moment of her *fiat* Mary began to carry all of us in her womb," the maternal vocation and mission of the Virgin toward those who believe in Christ actually began when Jesus said to her: "Woman, behold your son!" (Jn 19:26).

Homily, November 29, 2006

68. Imitation of Mary

I RECOMMEND that you love the Mother of the Lord. Do as St. John did, welcoming her deeply into your own heart. Allow yourselves to be continually renewed by her maternal love. Learn from her how to love Christ.

Homily, May 15, 2005

69. Sorrowful Mother

ONE must remain in prayer with Mary, the Mother given to us by Christ from the Cross.

Homily, October 19, 2005

70. Spiritual Mother

MARY is the *Spiritual Mother of all humanity,* because Jesus on the Cross shed His Blood for all of us and from the Cross He entrusted us all to her maternal care.

Homily, January 1, 2007

71. Pierced by the Spear

MARY Most Holy, who followed Jesus with total faith when He set out with determination for Jerusalem, to suffer the Passion . . . received like a "fresh skin" the "new wine" brought by the Son for the messianic betrothal (cf. Mk 2:22).

And so it was that the grace she requested with a motherly instinct for the spouses at Cana, she herself had first received beneath the Cross, poured out from the pierced Heart of the Son, an incarnation of God's love for humanity (cf. *Deus Caritas Est,* 13-15).

Angelus, February 26, 2006

72. Mary's Heart

IN the Heart of the Redeemer we adore God's love for humanity, His will for universal salvation, His infinite mercy. . . . The heart that resembles that of Christ more than any other is without a doubt the Heart of Mary, His Immaculate Mother.

Angelus, June 5, 2005

73. Mother of the Church

MARY, present on Calvary beneath the Cross, is also present with the Church and as Mother of the Church in each one of our Eucharistic Celebrations (cf. *Ecclesia de Eucharistia*, 57). No one better than she, therefore, can teach us to understand and live Holy Mass with faith and love, uniting ourselves with Christ's redeeming sacrifice.

When we receive Holy Communion, like Mary and united to her, we too clasp the wood that Jesus with His love transformed into an instrument of salvation, and pronounce our "Amen," our "Yes" to Love, crucified and risen.

Angelus, September 11, 2005

74. Our Lady of Holy Saturday

ON *Holy Saturday* the Church, spiritually united with Mary, remains in prayer at the tomb, where the Body of the Son of God is lying inert as it were in a condition of repose after the creative work of redemption brought about with His death (cf. Heb 4:1-13).

General Audience, April 12, 2006

75. Following Jesus

MARY is a woman who loves. How could it be otherwise? As a believer who in faith thinks with God's thoughts and wills with God's will, she cannot fail to be a woman who loves. We sense this in her quiet gestures, as recounted by the infancy narratives in the Gospel.

We see it in the delicacy with which she recognizes the need of the spouses at Cana and makes it known to Jesus. We see it in the humility with which she recedes into the background during Jesus' public life, knowing that the Son must establish a new family and that the Mother's hour will come only with the Cross, which will be Jesus' true hour (cf. Jn 2:4; 13:1).

When the disciples flee, Mary will remain beneath the Cross (cf. Jn 19:25-27); later, at the hour of Pentecost, it will be they who gather around her as they wait for the Holy Spirit (cf. Acts 1:14).

Deus Caritas Est, 41

7. Pentecost

76. Woman of the Eucharist

OUR Lady accompanies us every day in our prayers. . . . In his last Encyclical, *Ecclesia de Eucharistia,* our beloved Pope John Paul II presented her to us as "Woman of the Eucharist" throughout her life (cf. 53). "Woman of the Eucharist" through and through, beginning with her inner disposition: from the Annunciation, when she offered herself for the Incarnation of the Word of God, to the Cross and to the Resurrection; "Woman of the Eucharist" in the period subsequent to Pentecost, when she received in the Sacrament that Body that she had conceived and carried in her womb.

Address, May 31, 2005

77. The Upper Room

IN the Upper Room the Apostles did not know what awaited them. They were afraid and worried about their own future. They continued to marvel at the death and Resurrection of Jesus and were in anguish at being left on their own after His Ascension into heaven. Mary, "she who believed in the fulfillment of the Lord's words" (cf. Lk 1:45), assiduous in prayer alongside the Apostles, taught perseverance in the faith.

By her own attitude she convinced them that the Holy Spirit, in His wisdom, knew well the path on which He was leading them, and that consequently they could place their confidence in God, giving themselves to Him unreservedly, with their talents, their limitations, and their future.

Address, May 26, 2006

78. The Mystery of Pentecost

WE contemplate [the Virgin Mary] in the glorious mystery of Pentecost. The Holy Spirit, Who at Nazareth descended upon her to make her the Mother of the Word Incarnate (cf. Lk 1:35), descended . . . on the nascent Church joined together around her in the Upper Room (cf. Acts 1:14).

We invoke with trust Mary Most Holy, in order to obtain a renewed outpouring of the Spirit on the Church in our days.

Regina Caeli, May 15, 2005

79. The Virgin of the Upper Room

FOR Christians, as in the Upper Room, the Blessed Virgin always constitutes the living memorial of Jesus. It is she who enlivens their prayers and sustains their hope.

Let us ask her to guide us on our daily journey and to protect with special love those Christian communities that live in conditions of greater difficulty and suffering.

Angelus, March 26, 2006

80. Mother and Teacher

IN the days that followed the Lord's Resurrection, the Apostles stayed together, comforted by Mary's presence, and after the Ascension they persevered with her in prayerful expectation of Pentecost. Our Lady was a mother and teacher to them, a role that she continues to play for Christians of all times.

Every year, at Eastertide, we relive this experience more intensely and perhaps, precisely for this reason, popular tradition has dedicated to Mary the month of May that normally falls between Easter and Pentecost. Consequently, this month . . . helps us to rediscover the maternal role that she plays in our lives so that we may always be docile disciples and courageous witnesses of the Risen Lord.

Angelus, April 30, 2006

81. Mary and the Trinity

THE Virgin Mary, among all creatures, is a masterpiece of the Most Holy Trinity. In her humble heart full of faith, God prepared a worthy dwelling place for Himself in order to bring to completion the mystery of salvation. Divine Love found perfect correspondence in her, and in her womb the Only-begotten Son was made man.

Let us turn to Mary with filial trust, so that with her help we may progress in love and make our life a hymn of praise to the Father through the Son in the Holy Spirit.

Angelus, June 11, 2006

8. The Assumption

82. The Heart of Heaven

MARY was taken up body and soul into heaven: there is even room in God for the body. Heaven is no longer a very remote sphere unknown to us. We have a mother in heaven. And the Mother of God, the Mother of the Son of God, is our Mother. He Himself has said so.

He made her our Mother when He said to the disciple and to all of us: "Behold, your Mother!" We have a Mother in heaven. Heaven is open, heaven has a heart. *Homily,* August 15, 2005

83. Closeness

MARY is taken up body and soul into the glory of heaven, and with God and in God she is Queen of Heaven and earth. And is she really so remote from us? The contrary is true. Precisely because she is with God and in God, she is very close to each one of us.

While she lived on this earth she could only be close to a few people. Being in God, Who is close to us, actually, "within" all of us, Mary shares in this closeness of God. Being in God and with God, she is close to each one of us, knows our hearts, can hear our prayers, can help us with her motherly kindness, and has been given to us, as the Lord said, precisely as a "mother" to whom we can turn at every moment.

She always listens to us, she is always close to us, and being Mother of the Son, participates in the power of the Son and in his goodness. We can always entrust the whole of our lives to this Mother, who is not far from any one of us.

Homily, August 15, 2005

84. The Things Above

MARY is an example and support for all believers: she encourages us not to lose confidence before the difficulties and inevitable problems of every day. She assures us of her help and reminds us that it is essential to seek and think of "the things above, not those of the earth" (cf. Col 3:2).

Caught up in daily activities we risk, in fact, thinking that here, in this world in which we are only passing through, is the ultimate goal of human existence. Instead, Paradise is the true goal of our earthly pilgrimage.

How different our days would be if they were animated by this perspective! It was this way for the Saints. Their lives witnessed to what they lived, with their hearts continually directed to God. Earthly realities are lived properly because the eternal truth of divine love illuminates them.

Angelus, August 15, 2006

85. Gate of Heaven

HEAVEN is our final dwelling place; from there, Mary encourages us by her example to welcome God's will, so as not to allow ourselves to be seduced by the deceptive attraction to what is transitory and fleeting, and not to give in to the temptations of selfishness and evil that extinguish the joy of life in the heart.

Angelus, August 15, 2005

86. Mary and the Holy Spirit

THUS, full light is shed on the bond that united Mary with the Holy Spirit from the very beginning of her existence when, as she was being conceived, the Spirit, the eternal Love of the Father and of the Son, made His dwelling within her and preserved her from any shadow of sin; then again, when the same Spirit brought the Son of God into being in her womb; and yet again when, with the grace of the Spirit, Mary's own words were fulfilled through the whole span of her life: "Behold, I am the handmaid of the Lord"; and lastly, when, by the power of the Holy Spirit, Mary was taken up physically to be beside the Son in the glory of God the Father.

Address, May 1, 2006

9. Marian Devotion

87. Homage to Mary

IN contemplating the face of Christ, and in Christ, the face of the Father, Mary Most Holy precedes, sustains, and accompanies us. Love and devotion for the Mother of the Lord, so widespread and deeply rooted in the Italian People, are a precious heritage that we must always nurture and a great resource in view of evangelization.

Address, May 30, 2005

88. Church of Mary

MAY the Virgin Mary, so loved and venerated in every part of Italy, precede and guide us in our union with Christ. In her we meet, pure and undeformed, the true essence of the Church, and so through her, we learn to know and love the mystery of the Church that lives in history, we deeply feel a part of it, and in our turn we become "ecclesial souls," we learn to resist that "internal secularization" that threatens the Church of our time, a consequence of the secularization process that has profoundly marked European civilization.

Address, October 19, 2006

89. Veneration of Mary

TRUE Marian devotion never obscures or diminishes faith and love for Jesus Christ Our Savior, the one Mediator between God and humankind. On the contrary, entrustment to Our Lady is a privileged path, tested by numerous Saints, for a more faithful following of the Lord.

Consequently, let us entrust ourselves to her with filial abandonment!

Address, May 31, 2006

90. Mother Most Pure

LOOKING at Mary, how can we, her children, fail to let the aspiration to beauty, goodness, and purity of heart be aroused in us?

Her heavenly candor draws us to God, helping us to overcome the temptation to live a mediocre life composed of compromises with evil, and directs us decisively toward the authentic good that is the source of joy.

Angelus, December 8, 2005

91. Mother Most Amiable

MEN and women . . . constantly experience the gift of Mary's goodness and the unfailing love that she pours out from the depths of her heart. The testimonials of gratitude, offered to her from every continent and culture, are a recognition of that pure love that is not self-seeking but simply benevolent.

At the same time, the devotion of the faithful shows an infallible intuition of how such love is possible: it becomes so as a result of the most intimate union with God, through which the soul is totally pervaded by Him—a condition that enables those who have drunk from the fountain of God's love to become in their turn a fountain from which "flow rivers of living water" (Jn 7:38).

Mary, Virgin and Mother, shows us what love is and whence it draws its origin and its constantly renewed power. To her we entrust the Church and her mission in the service of love.

Deus Caritas Est, 42

92. Mother of Consolation

THE closer a person is to God, the closer he is to people. We see this in Mary. The fact that she is totally with God is the reason why she is so close to human beings.

For this reason she can be the Mother of every consolation and every help, a Mother whom anyone can dare to address in any kind of need in weakness and in sin, for she has understanding for everything and is for everyone the open power of creative goodness.

Homily, December 8, 2005

93. Our Lady of Lourdes

WE all know that the Virgin expressed God's tenderness for the suffering in the Grotto of Massabielle. This tenderness, this loving concern, is felt in an especially lively way in the world precisely on the day of the Feast of Our Lady of Lourdes, re-presenting in the liturgy, and especially in the Eucharist, the mystery of Christ, Redeemer of Man, of whom the Immaculate Virgin is the first fruit.

In presenting herself to Bernadette as the Immaculate Conception, Mary Most Holy came to remind the modern world, which was in danger of forgetting it, of the primacy of divine grace that is stronger than sin and death.

Address, February 11, 2006

94. Our Lady of Mount Carmel

THE Carmelites have spread among the Christian people devotion to Our Lady of Mount Carmel, holding her up as a model of prayer, contemplation, and dedication to God.

Indeed, Mary was the first, in a way that can never be equaled, to believe and experience that Jesus, the Incarnate Word, is the summit, the peak of man's encounter with God. By fully accepting the Word, she "was blessedly brought to the holy Mountain" (cf. *Opening Prayer of the Memorial*), and lives for ever with the Lord in body and soul.

Angelus, July 16, 2006

95. Seat of Wisdom

[LET us] learn from the Virgin Mary, the first person to contemplate the humanity of the Incarnate Word, the humanity of Divine Wisdom.

In the Baby Jesus, with Whom she had infinite and silent conversations, she recognized the human Face of God, so that the mysterious Wisdom of the Son was impressed on the Mother's mind and heart. So it was that Mary became the "Seat of Wisdom."

Address, December 14, 2006

96. Queen of Martyrs

MARY, who held the Redeemer in her arms at Bethlehem, also suffers an interior martyrdom herself. She shared His Passion and had to take Him yet again in her arms when He was taken down from the Cross.

To this Mother, who knew the joy of His birth and the torment of the death of her divine Son, we entrust all those who are persecuted and suffering in various ways for their witness and service to the Gospel.

Angelus, December 26, 2006

97. Queen of the Most Holy Rosary

CELEBRATING the feast of Our Lady of the Rosary . . . it is as though Our Lady invites us every year to rediscover the beauty of this prayer, so simple and so profound.

Angelus, October 1, 2006

98. Queen of the Family

MARY . . . is a prefiguration of the Mother who protects by her love God's family on its earthly pilgrimage. Mary is the image and model of all mothers, of their great mission to be guardians of life, of their mission to be teachers of the art of living and of the art of loving.

Homily, July 9, 2006

99. Queen of the Church

THE icon of the Annunciation, more than any other, helps us to see clearly how everything in the Church goes back to that mystery of Mary's acceptance of the divine Word, by which, through the action of the Holy Spirit, the Covenant between God and humanity was perfectly sealed.

Everything in the Church, every institution and ministry, including that of Peter and his Successors, is "included" under the Virgin's mantle, within the grace-filled horizon of her "yes" to God's will.

Homily, March 25, 2006

100. Personal Praise to Mary

I WOULD also like to express to Mary my gratitude for the support she offers me in my daily service to the Church.

I know that I can count on her help in every situation; indeed, I know that she foresees with maternal intuition all her children's needs and intervenes effectively to sustain them: this has been the experience of the Christian people ever since its first steps in Jerusalem.

Address, May 31, 2006

10. Prayers to Mary

Prayer to Mary (I)

WE want to thank you, Virgin Mother of God and our most beloved Mother, for your intercession for the good of the Church. You, who in embracing the divine will without reserve were consecrated with all of your energies to the person and work of your Son, teach us to keep in our heart and to meditate in silence, as you did, upon the mysteries of Christ's life.

May you who reached Calvary, ever-deeply united to your Son Who from the Cross gave you as mother to the disciple John, also make us feel you are always close in each moment of our lives, especially in times of darkness and trial.

You, who at Pentecost, together with the Apostles in prayer, called upon the gift of the Holy Spirit for the newborn Church, help us to persevere in the faithful following of Christ. To you, a "sign of certain hope and comfort," we trustfully turn our gaze "until the day of the Lord shall come" (*Lumen Gentium*, 68).

You, Mary, are invoked with the insistent prayer of the faithful throughout the world so that you, exalted above all the Angels and Saints, will intercede before your Son for us, "until all families of peoples, whether they are honored with the title of Christian or whether they still do not know the Savior, may be happily gathered together in peace and harmony into one People of God, for the glory of the Most Holy and Undivided Trinity" (*Lumen Gentium*, 69). Amen.

Address, December 8, 2005

Prayer to Mary (II)

HOLY Mary, Mother of God,
you have given the world its true light,
Jesus, your Son—the Son of God.
You abandoned yourself completely
to God's call
and thus became a wellspring
of the goodness which flows forth from Him.
Show us Jesus. Lead us to Him.
Teach us to know and love Him,
so that we too can become
capable of true love
and be fountains of living water
in the midst of a thirsting world.

Deus Caritas Est, 42

Prayer to Mary (III)

YOUR Son, just before His farewell to His disciples, said to them: "Whoever wishes to become great among you must be your servant, and whoever wishes to be first among you must be slave of all" (Mk 10:43-44). At the decisive hour in your own life, you said: "I am the servant of the Lord" (Lk 1:38).

You lived your whole life as service. And you continue to do so throughout history. At Cana, you silently and discreetly interceded for the spouses, and so you continue to do. You take upon yourself people's needs and concerns, and you bring them before the Lord, before your Son. Your power is goodness. Your power is service.

Teach us—great and small alike—to carry out our responsibilities in the same way. Help us to find the strength to offer reconciliation and forgiveness. Help us to become patient and humble, but also free and courageous, just as you were at the hour of the Cross. In your arms you hold Jesus, the Child Who blesses, the Child Who is also the Lord of the world.

By holding the Child Who blesses, you have yourself become a blessing. Bless us, this city and this country! Show us Jesus, the blessed fruit of your womb! Pray for us sinners, now and at the hour of our death. Amen!

Prayer, September 9, 2006

Prayer to Mary (IV)

"*F*ULL *of grace*" are you, Mary, full of divine love from the very first moment of your existence, providentially predestined to be Mother of the Redeemer and intimately connected to Him in the mystery of salvation. In your Immaculate Conception shines forth the vocation of Christ's disciples, called to become, with His grace, Saints and immaculate through love (cf. Eph 1:4). In you shines the dignity of every human being who is always precious in the Creator's eyes.

Those who look to you, All Holy Mother, never lose their serenity, no matter what the hardships of life. Although the experience of sin is a sad one since it disfigures the dignity of God's children, anyone who turns to you discovers the beauty of truth and love and finds the path that leads to the Father's house.

"Full of grace" are you, Mary, who, welcoming with your "yes" the Creator's plan, opened to us the path of salvation. Teach us also at your school to say our "yes" to the Lord's will. Let it be a "yes" that joins with your own "yes," without reservations or shadows, a "yes" that the Heavenly Father willed to have need of in order to beget the new Man, Christ, the one Savior of the world and of history. Give us the courage to

say "no" to the deceptions of power, money, pleasure; to dishonest earnings, corruption, and hypocrisy, to selfishness and violence; "no" to the Evil One, the deceitful prince of this world; to say "yes" to Christ, who destroys the power of evil with the omnipotence of love. We know that only hearts converted to Love, which is God, can build a better future for all.

"Full of grace" are you, Mary! For all generations your name is a pledge of sure hope. Yes! Because as the great poet, Dante, wrote, for us mortals you are "a source of living hope" (*Paradise*, XXXIII, 12). Let us come once again as trusting pilgrims to draw faith and comfort, joy and love, safety and peace from this source, the wellspring of your Immaculate Heart.

Virgin "full of grace," show yourself to be a tender and caring Mother to those who live in this city of yours, so that the true Gospel spirit may enliven and guide their conduct; show yourself as Mother and watchful keeper of Italy and Europe, so that people may draw from their ancient Christian roots fresh vigor to build their present and their future; show yourself as a provident and merciful Mother to the whole world so that, by respecting human dignity and rejecting every form of violence and exploitation, sound foundations may be laid for the civilization of love.

Show yourself as Mother, especially to those most in need: the defenseless, the marginalized and outcasts, to the victims of a society that all too often sacrifices the human person for other ends and interests.

Show yourself, O Mary, as Mother of all, and give us Christ, the Hope of the world! *"Show yourself as a Mother, oh Virgin full of grace,"* O Virgin Immaculate, full of grace! Amen!

Prayer, December 8, 2006

Prayer to Mary (V)

LET us entrust to Mary, who is the Mother of Mercy incarnate, particularly those situations to which the Lord's grace alone can bring peace, comfort, and justice.

The Virgin heard the Angel announcing her divine Motherhood say to her: "With God nothing will be impossible" (Lk 1:37). Mary believed and for this reason she is blessed (cf. Lk 1:45). What is impossible to man becomes possible to the one who believes (cf. Mk 9:23).

Thus . . . let us ask the Mother of God to obtain for us the gift of a mature faith: a faith that we would like to resemble hers as far as possible, a clear, genuine, humble, and at the same time courageous faith, steeped in hope and enthusiasm for the Kingdom of God, a faith devoid of all fatalism and wholly set on cooperating with the divine will in full and joyful obedience and with the absolute certainty that God wants nothing but love and life, always and for everyone.

Obtain for us, O Mary, an authentic, pure faith. May you always be thanked and blessed, Holy Mother of God! Amen!

Homily, December 31, 2006

ANALYTICAL INDEX

(The reference is to the numbers of each thought.)